SPIRIT
of
FAITH

OBEDIENCE
to GOD

SPIRIT
of
FAITH

OBEDIENCE
to GOD

compiled by Bahá'í Publishing

Bahá'í
PUBLISHING
Wilmette, Illinois

Bahá'í Publishing
415 Linden Avenue, Wilmette, Illinois 60091-2844
Copyright © 2012 by the National Spiritual Assembly
of the Bahá'ís of the United States

15   14   13   12   4   3   2   1

Library of Congress Cataloging-in-Publication Data

Spirit of faith : obedience to God / compiled by Baha'i
Publishing.
   p. cm.
 Includes bibliographical references (p. 137).
 ISBN 978-1-61851-019-8 (alk. paper)
 1. Bahai Faith—Doctrines. 2. Obedience—Religious
aspects—Bahai Faith. I. Baha'i Publishing.
 BP370.S65 2012
 297.9'32—dc23

                        2012021251

Cover design by Andrew Johnson
Book design by Patrick Falso

CONTENTS

INTRODUCTION

Obedience to God is the fifth book in Bahá'í Publishing's *Spirit of Faith* series, which continues to explore weighty spiritual topics—including the oneness of mankind, the unity of the world's religions, and the promise of world peace—by taking an in-depth look at how the writings of the Bahá'í Faith address these issues. It is hoped that meditation on the passages presented here will lead to profound and rewarding conversations.

The Bahá'í Faith is an independent world religion that began in 1844 in Persia (present-day Iran). Since its inception, the Bahá'í Faith has spread to 235 nations and territories and has been accepted by more than five million people. Bahá'ís believe that there is only one God, that all the major world religions come from God, and that all the members of the human race are essentially members of one family. Bahá'ís strive to eliminate all forms of prejudice and believe that people of all races, nations, social status, and religious backgrounds are equal in the sight of God. The Bahá'í Faith also teaches that each individual is responsible for the independent investigation of truth, that science and religion are in harmony, and that men and women are equal in the sight of God.

Collected in this volume are a series of passages related to the subject of obedience—a virtue that is given prominence and insightful analysis in the Bahá'í writings. Bahá'u'lláh, the Faith's Founder, describes His commandments as "the lamps of My loving providence among My servants, and the keys of My mercy for My creatures," and states that "true liberty consisteth in man's submission unto My commandments." From a Bahá'í perspective, the Prophets or Manifestations of God, the Founders of the world's great religions, are as divine Physicians Whose laws, teachings, and admonitions contain the remedy for the ailments of mankind. To follow the teachings and observe the laws prescribed by the Manifestation of God for the day in which we live is, from a Bahá'í perspective, to fulfill our duty as human beings and to align ourselves with the divine guidance available to us. From this perspective, obedience can be seen as a source of empowerment and as the core of personal spiritual development. Included in this book are the writings of Bahá'u'lláh, the Founder of the Bahá'í Faith, considered by Bahá'ís to be the supreme Manifestation of God for the age in which we live; the writings of His forerunner, the

Báb; and the writings and recorded utterances of His son and appointed successor, 'Abdu'l-Bahá. It is hoped that readers of all faiths and backgrounds will find the passages collected here to be thought-provoking and inspiring, and that meditation on this subject will lead to new insights and understandings.

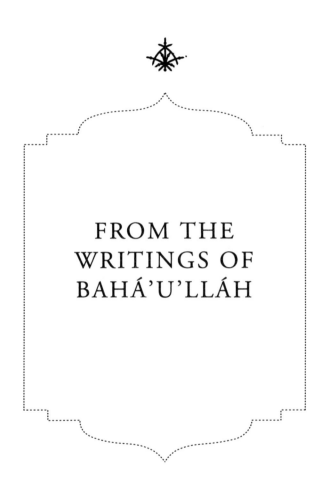

FROM THE
WRITINGS OF
BAHÁ'U'LLÁH

1

O ye peoples of the world! Know assuredly that My commandments are the lamps of My loving providence among My servants, and the keys of My mercy for My creatures. Thus hath it been sent down from the heaven of the Will of your Lord, the Lord of Revelation. Were any man to taste the sweetness of the words which the lips of the All-Merciful have willed to utter, he would, though the treasures of the earth be in his possession, renounce them one and all, that he might

vindicate the truth of even one of His commandments, shining above the dayspring of His bountiful care and loving-kindness.

2

The first duty prescribed by God for His servants is the recognition of Him Who is the Dayspring of His Revelation and the Fountain of His laws, Who representeth the Godhead in both the Kingdom of His Cause and the world of creation. Whoso achieveth this duty hath attained unto all good; and whoso is deprived thereof hath gone astray, though he be the author of every righteous deed. It behooveth every one who reacheth this most sublime station, this summit of transcendent glory, to observe every ordinance of Him Who is the Desire of the world. These twin duties are inseparable. Neither is acceptable without the other. Thus hath it been decreed by Him Who is the Source of Divine inspiration.

From the Writings of Bahá'u'lláh   9

3

Where shalt thou secure the cord of thy faith and fasten the tie of thine obedience? By Him Who revealeth Himself in His oneness and Whose own Self beareth witness to His unity! Should there be ignited in thy heart the burning brand of the love of God, thou wouldst seek neither rest nor composure, neither laughter nor repose, but wouldst hasten to scale the highest summits in the realms of divine nearness, sanctity, and beauty.

4

What mankind needeth in this day is obedience unto them that are in authority, and a faithful adherence to the cord of wisdom.

5

In all these journeys the traveler must stray not the breadth of a hair from the "Law," for this is indeed the secret of the "Path" and the fruit of the Tree of "Truth"; and in all these stages he must cling to the robe of obedience to the commandments, and hold fast to the cord of shunning all forbidden things, that he may be nourished from the cup of the Law and informed of the mysteries of Truth.

6

O thou who treadest the path of justice and beholdest the countenance of mercy! Thine epistle was received, thy question was noted, and the sweet accents of thy soul were heard from the inmost chambers of thy heart. Whereupon the clouds of the Divine Will were raised to rain upon thee the outpourings of heavenly wisdom, to divest thee of all that thou hadst acquired aforetime, to draw thee from the realms of contradiction unto the retreats of oneness, and to lead thee to the sacred streams of His Law. Perchance thou mayest quaff therefrom, repose therein, quench thy thirst, refresh thy soul, and be numbered with those whom the light of God hath guided aright in this day.

7

Know verily that the essence of justice and the source thereof are both embodied in the ordinances prescribed by Him Who is the Manifestation of the Self of God amongst men, if ye be of them that recognize this truth. He doth verily incarnate the highest, the infallible standard of justice unto all creation. Were His law to be such as to strike terror into the hearts of all that are in heaven and on earth, that law is naught but manifest justice. The fears and agitation which the revelation of this law provokes in men's hearts should indeed be likened to the cries of the suckling babe weaned from his mother's milk, if ye be of them that perceive. Were men to discover the motivating purpose of God's Revelation, they would assuredly cast away their fears, and, with hearts filled with gratitude, rejoice with exceeding gladness.

8

Bear thou witness in thine inmost heart unto this testimony which God hath Himself and for Himself pronounced, that there is none other God but Him, that all else besides Him have been created by His behest, have been fashioned by His leave, are subject to His law, are as a thing forgotten when compared to the glorious evidences of His oneness, and are as nothing when brought face to face with the mighty revelations of His unity.

9

O kings of the earth! The Most Great Law hath been revealed in this Spot, this scene of transcendent splendor. Every hidden thing hath been brought to light, by virtue of the Will of the Supreme Ordainer, He Who hath ushered in the Last Hour, through Whom the Moon hath been cleft, and every irrevocable decree expounded.

10

Set thy heart firmly upon justice, and alter not the Cause of God, and be of them whose eyes are directed towards the things that have been revealed in His Book. Follow not, under any condition, the promptings of thine evil desires. Keep thou the law of God, thy Lord, the Beneficent, the Ancient of Days. Thou shalt most certainly return to dust, and shalt perish like all the things in which thou takest delight. This is what the Tongue of truth and glory hath spoken.

11

Thou art He through Whom the ensign "Praiseworthy art Thou in Thy works" hath been lifted up, and the standard "Obeyed art Thou in thy behest" hath been unfurled. Make known this Thy station, O my God, unto Thy servants, that they may be made aware that the excellence of all things is dependent upon Thy bidding and Thy word, and the virtue of every act is conditioned by Thy leave and the good pleasure of Thy will, and may recognize that the reins of men's doings are within the grasp of Thine acceptance and Thy commandment.

12

In the daytime and in the night season, at even and at morn, We pray to God on thy behalf, that He may graciously aid thee to be obedient unto Him and to observe His commandment, that He may shield thee from the hosts of the evil ones. Do, therefore, as it pleaseth thee, and treat Us as befitteth thy station and beseemeth thy sovereignty. Be not forgetful of the law of God in whatever thou desirest to achieve, now or in the days to come. Say: Praise be to God, the Lord of all worlds!

13

Gird up the loins of thine endeavor, that happily thou mayest guide thy neighbor to the law of God, the Most Merciful. Such an act, verily, excelleth all other acts in the sight of God, the All-Possessing, the Most High. Such must be thy steadfastness in the Cause of God, that no earthly thing whatsoever will have the power to deter thee from thy duty. Though the powers of earth be leagued against thee, though all men dispute with thee, thou must remain unshaken.

14

Glorified be Thou, then, O my God! I beseech Thee by Thy Most Great Name to assemble them that love Thee around the Law that streameth from the good-pleasure of Thy will, and to send down upon them what will assure their hearts.

15

Praised be Thou, O Lord my God! I implore Thee by Them Who are the Tabernacles of Thy Divine holiness, Who are the Manifestations of Thy transcendent unity and the Daysprings of Thine inspiration and revelation, to grant that Thy servants may not be kept back from this Divine Law which, at Thy will and according to Thy pleasure, hath branched out from Thy most great Ocean. Do Thou, then, ordain for them that which Thou didst ordain for Thy chosen ones and for the righteous among Thy creatures, whose constancy in Thy Cause the tempests of trials have failed to shake, and whom the tumults of tests have been powerless to hinder from magnifying Thy most exalted Word—the Word through Which the heavens of men's idle fancies and vain imaginations have been split asunder. Thou art, verily, the Almighty, the All-Glorious, the All-Knowing.

16

I beseech Thee, by Thy Most Great Name, to open the eyes of Thy servants, that they may behold Thee shining above the horizon of Thy majesty and glory, and that they may not be hindered by the croaking of the raven from hearkening to the voice of the Dove of Thy sublime oneness, nor be prevented by the corrupt waters from partaking of the pure wine of Thy bounty and the everlasting streams of Thy gifts.

Gather them, then, together around this Divine Law, the covenant of which Thou hast established with all Thy Prophets and Thy Messengers, and Whose ordinances Thou hast written down in

Thy Tablets and Thy Scriptures. Raise them up, moreover, to such heights as will enable them to perceive Thy Call.

Potent art Thou to do what pleaseth Thee. Thou art, verily, the Inaccessible, the All-Glorious.

17

The purpose of religion as revealed from the heaven of God's holy Will is to establish unity and concord amongst the peoples of the world; make it not the cause of dissension and strife. The religion of God and His divine law are the most potent instruments and the surest of all means for the dawning of the light of unity amongst men. The progress of the world, the development of nations, the tranquility of peoples, and the peace of all who dwell on earth are among the principles and ordinances of God. Religion bestoweth upon man the most precious of all gifts, offereth the cup of prosperity, imparteth eternal life, and showereth imperishable benefits upon mankind.

From the Writings of Bahá'u'lláh 27

18

Consider the hardships and the bitterness of the lives of those Revealers of the divine Beauty. Reflect, how single-handed and alone they faced the world and all its peoples, and promulgated the Law of God! No matter how severe the persecutions inflicted upon those holy, those precious, and tender Souls, they still remained, in the plenitude of their power, patient, and, despite their ascendancy, they suffered and endured.

19

Give ear, O peoples of the earth, unto that which the Pen of the Lord of all nations commandeth you. Know ye of a certainty that the Dispensations of the past have attained their highest, their final consummation in the Law that hath branched out from this Most Great Ocean. Haste ye thereunto at Our behest. We, verily, ordain as We please. Regard ye the world as a man's body, which is afflicted with divers ailments, and the recovery of which dependeth upon the harmonizing of all of its component elements. Gather ye around that which We have prescribed unto you, and walk not in the ways of such as create dissension.

20

That the divers communions of the earth, and the manifold systems of religious belief, should never be allowed to foster the feelings of animosity among men, is, in this Day, of the essence of the Faith of God and His Religion. These principles and laws, these firmly-established and mighty systems, have proceeded from one Source, and are rays of one Light. That they differ one from another is to be attributed to the varying requirements of the ages in which they were promulgated.

21

If thou be of the inmates of this city within the ocean of divine unity, thou wilt view all the Prophets and Messengers of God as one soul and one body, as one light and one spirit, in such wise that the first among them would be last and the last would be first. For they have all arisen to proclaim His Cause and have established the laws of divine wisdom. They are, one and all, the Manifestations of His Self, the Repositories of His might, the Treasuries of His Revelation, the Dawning-Places of His splendor and the Daysprings of His light.

22

Say: It behooveth you, O Ministers of State, to keep the precepts of God, and to forsake your own laws and regulations, and to be of them who are guided aright. Better is this for you than all ye possess, did ye but know it. If ye transgress the commandment of God, not one jot or one tittle of all your works shall be acceptable in His sight. Ye shall, erelong, discover the consequences of that which ye shall have done in this vain life, and shall be repaid for them. This, verily, is the truth, the undoubted truth.

23

By Him Who holdeth in His grasp the kingdom of the entire creation! Nowhere doth your true and abiding glory reside except in your firm adherence unto the precepts of God, your wholehearted observance of His laws, your resolution to see that they do not remain unenforced, and to pursue steadfastly the right course.

24

I render Thee thanks, O Thou Who hast lighted Thy fire within my soul, and cast the beams of Thy light into my heart, that Thou hast taught Thy servants how to make mention of Thee, and revealed unto them the ways whereby they can supplicate Thee, through Thy most holy and exalted tongue, and Thy most august and precious speech. But for Thy leave, who is there that could venture to express Thy might and Thy grandeur; and were it not for Thine instruction, who is the man that could discover the ways of Thy pleasure in the kingdom of Thy creation?

25

A twofold obligation resteth upon him who hath recognized the Dayspring of the Unity of God, and acknowledged the truth of Him Who is the Manifestation of His oneness. The first is steadfastness in His love, such steadfastness that neither the clamor of the enemy nor the claims of the idle pretender can deter him from cleaving unto Him Who is the Eternal Truth, a steadfastness that taketh no account of them whatever. The second is strict observance of the laws He hath prescribed—laws which He hath always ordained, and will continue to ordain, unto men, and through which the truth may be distinguished and separated from falsehood.

26

All the atoms of the earth bear witness, O my Lord, to the greatness of Thy power and of Thy sovereignty; and all the signs of the universe attest the glory of Thy majesty and of Thy might. Have mercy, then, O Thou Who art the sovereign Lord of all, Who art the King of everlasting days, and Ruler of all nations, upon these Thy servants, who have clung to the cord of Thy commandments, who have bowed their necks to the revelations of Thy laws which have been sent down from the heaven of Thy Will.

27

Think not that We have revealed unto you a mere code of laws. Nay, rather, We have unsealed the choice Wine with the fingers of might and power. To this beareth witness that which the Pen of Revelation hath revealed. Meditate upon this, O men of insight!

28

Whenever My laws appear like the sun in the heaven of Mine utterance, they must be faithfully obeyed by all, though My decree be such as to cause the heaven of every religion to be cleft asunder. He doth what He pleaseth. He chooseth; and none may question His choice. Whatsoever He, the Well-Beloved, ordaineth, the same is, verily, beloved. To this He Who is the Lord of all creation beareth Me witness. Whoso hath inhaled the sweet fragrance of the All-Merciful, and recognized the Source of this utterance, will welcome with his own eyes the shafts of the enemy, that he may establish the truth of the laws of God amongst men. Well is it with him that hath turned thereunto, and apprehended the meaning of His decisive decree.

29

In formulating the principles and laws a part hath been devoted to penalties which form an effective instrument for the security and protection of men. However, dread of the penalties maketh people desist only outwardly from committing vile and contemptible deeds, while that which guardeth and restraineth man both outwardly and inwardly hath been and still is the fear of God. It is man's true protector and his spiritual guardian. It behooveth him to cleave tenaciously unto that which will lead to the appearance of this supreme bounty. Well is it with him who giveth ear unto whatsoever My Pen of Glory hath proclaimed and observeth that whereunto he is bidden by the Ordainer, the Ancient of Days.

30

We have revealed Ourself unto men, have unveiled the Cause, guided all mankind towards God's Straight Path, promulgated the laws and have enjoined upon everyone that which shall truly profit them both in this world and in the next.

31

Say: From My laws the sweet-smelling savor of My garment can be smelled, and by their aid the standards of Victory will be planted upon the highest peaks. The Tongue of My power hath, from the heaven of My omnipotent glory, addressed to My creation these words: "Observe My commandments, for the love of My beauty." Happy is the lover that hath inhaled the divine fragrance of his Best-Beloved from these words, laden with the perfume of a grace which no tongue can describe. By My life! He who hath drunk the choice wine of fairness from the hands of My bountiful favor will circle around My commandments that shine above the Dayspring of My creation.

32

Glorified be Thy name, O Lord my God! I beseech Thee by Thy power that hath encompassed all created things, and by Thy Sovereignty that hath transcended the entire creation, and by Thy Word which was hidden in Thy wisdom and whereby Thou didst create Thy heaven and Thy earth, both to enable us to be steadfast in our love for Thee and in our obedience to Thy pleasure, and to fix our gaze upon Thy face, and celebrate Thy glory. Empower us, then, O my God, to spread abroad Thy signs among Thy creatures, and to guard Thy Faith in Thy realm. Thou hast ever existed independently of the mention of any of Thy creatures, and wilt remain as Thou hast been for ever and ever.

In Thee I have placed my whole confidence, unto Thee I have turned my face, to the cord of Thy loving providence I have clung, and towards the shadow of Thy mercy I have hastened. Cast me not as one disappointed out of Thy door, O my God, and withhold not from me Thy grace, for Thee alone do I seek. No God is there beside Thee, the Ever-Forgiving, the Most Bountiful.

Praise be to Thee, O Thou Who art the Beloved of them that have known thee!

33

Observe ye the injunctions laid upon you by Him Who is the Dawning-place of Utterance. The sincere among His servants will regard the precepts set forth by God as the Water of Life to the followers of every faith, and the Lamp of wisdom and loving providence to all the denizens of earth and heaven.

34

We school you with the rod of wisdom and laws, like unto the father who educateth his son, and this for naught but the protection of your own selves and the elevation of your stations. By My life, were ye to discover what We have desired for you in revealing Our holy laws, ye would offer up your very souls for this sacred, this mighty, and most exalted Faith.

35

O Most Mighty Ocean! Sprinkle upon the nations that with which Thou hast been charged by Him Who is the Sovereign of Eternity, and adorn the temples of all the dwellers of the earth with the vesture of His laws through which all hearts will rejoice and all eyes be brightened.

36

To enforce the laws of God is naught but justice, and is the source of universal content. Nay more, the divine statutes have always been, and will ever remain, the cause and instrument of the preservation of mankind, as witnessed by His exalted words: "In punishment will ye find life, O men of insight!"

37

Say: From My laws the sweet smelling savor of My garment can be smelled, and by their aid the standards of victory will be planted upon the highest peaks. The Tongue of My power hath, from the heaven of My omnipotent glory, addressed to My creation these words: "Observe My commandments, for the love of My beauty." Happy is the lover that hath inhaled the divine fragrance of his Best-Beloved from these words, laden with the perfume of a grace which no tongue can describe. By My life! He who hath drunk the choice wine of fairness from the hands of My bountiful favor, will circle around My commandments that shine above the Dayspring of My creation.

38

Were the mysteries, that are known to none except God, to be unraveled, the whole of mankind would witness the evidences of perfect and consummate justice. With a certitude that none can question, all men would cleave to His commandments, and would scrupulously observe them.

39

The ordinances of God have been sent down from the heaven of His most august Revelation. All must diligently observe them. Man's supreme distinction, his real advancement, his final victory, have always depended, and will continue to depend, upon them. Whoso keepeth the commandments of God shall attain everlasting felicity.

40

Say: Beware, . . . lest ye walk in the ways of them whose words differ from their deeds. Strive that ye may be enabled to manifest to the peoples of the earth the signs of God, and to mirror forth His commandments. Let your acts be a guide unto all mankind, for the professions of most men, be they high or low, differ from their conduct. It is through your deeds that ye can distinguish yourselves from others. Through them the brightness of your light can be shed upon the whole earth. Happy is the man that heedeth My counsel, and keepeth the precepts prescribed by Him Who is the All-Knowing, the All-Wise.

41

Say: True liberty consisteth in man's submission unto My commandments, little as ye know it. Were men to observe that which We have sent down unto them from the Heaven of Revelation, they would, of a certainty, attain unto perfect liberty. Happy is the man that hath apprehended the Purpose of God in whatever He hath revealed from the Heaven of His Will, that pervadeth all created things. Say: The liberty that profiteth you is to be found nowhere except in complete servitude unto God, the Eternal Truth. Whoso hath tasted of its sweetness will refuse to barter it for all the dominion of earth and heaven.

42

It is incumbent upon everyone to observe God's holy commandments, inasmuch as they are the wellspring of life unto the world. The heaven of divine wisdom is illumined with the two luminaries of consultation and compassion and the canopy of world order is upraised upon the two pillars of reward and punishment.

43

Moreover, We announce unto everyone the joyful tidings concerning that which We have revealed in Our Most Holy Book—a Book from above whose horizon the daystar of My commandments shineth upon every observer and every observed one. Hold ye fast unto it and fulfill that which is revealed therein. Indeed better is this for you than whatsoever hath been created in the world, did ye but know it. Beware lest the transitory things of human life withhold you from turning unto God, the True One.

44

O SON OF MAN!
Neglect not My commandments if thou lovest My beauty, and forget not My counsels if thou wouldst attain My good pleasure.

45

The essence of wisdom is the fear of God, the dread of His scourge and punishment, and the apprehension of His justice and decree.

FROM THE
WRITINGS OF
THE BÁB

1

There is no paradise, in the estimation of the believers in the Divine Unity, more exalted than to obey God's commandments, and there is no fire in the eyes of those who have known God and His signs, fiercer than to transgress His laws and to oppress another soul, even to the extent of a mustard seed.

2

How vast the number of people who are well versed in every science, yet it is their adherence to the holy Word of God which will determine their faith, inasmuch as the fruit of every science is none other than the knowledge of divine precepts and submission unto His good-pleasure.

3

O people of the earth! Whoso obeyeth the Remembrance of God and His Book hath in truth obeyed God and His chosen ones and he will, in the life to come, be reckoned in the presence of God among the inmates of the Paradise of His good-pleasure.

4

Since thou hast faithfully obeyed the true religion of God in the past, it behooveth thee to follow His true religion hereafter, inasmuch as every religion proceedeth from God, the Help in Peril, the Self-Subsisting.

5

They that truly believe in God and in His signs, and who in every Dispensation faithfully obey that which hath been revealed in the Book—such are indeed the ones whom God hath created from the fruits of the Paradise of His good-pleasure, and who are of the blissful.

6

Thou knowest full well, O my God, that tribulations have showered upon me from all directions and that no one can dispel or transmute them except Thee. I know of a certainty, by virtue of my love for Thee, that Thou wilt never cause tribulations to befall any soul unless Thou desirest to exalt his station in Thy earthly life with the bulwark of Thine all-compelling power, that it may not become inclined toward the vanities of this world. Indeed Thou art well aware that under all conditions I would cherish the remembrance of Thee far more than the ownership of all that is in the heavens and on the earth.

Strengthen my heart, O my God, in Thine obedience and in Thy love, and grant that I may be clear of the entire company of Thine adversaries. Verily, I swear by Thy glory that I yearn for naught besides Thyself, nor do I desire anything except Thy mercy, nor am I apprehensive of aught save Thy justice. I beg Thee to forgive me as well as those whom Thou lovest, howsoever Thou pleasest. Verily, Thou art the Almighty, the Bountiful.

Immensely exalted art Thou, O Lord of the heavens and earth, above the praise of all men, and may peace be upon Thy faithful servants and glory be unto God, the Lord of all the worlds.

FROM THE WRITINGS AND RECORDED UTTERANCES OF 'ABDU'L-BAHÁ

1

The Laws of God are not imposition of will, or of power, or pleasure, but the resolutions of truth, reason and justice.

2

I want to make you understand that material progress and spiritual progress are two very different things, and that only if material progress goes hand in hand with spirituality can any real progress come about, and the Most Great Peace reign in the world. If men followed the Holy Counsels and the Teachings of the Prophets, if Divine Light shone in all hearts and men were really religious, we should soon see peace on earth and the Kingdom of God among men. The laws of God may be likened unto the soul and material progress unto the body. If the body was not animated by the soul, it would cease to exist. It is my earnest prayer that spirituality may ever grow and increase in the

world, so that customs may become enlightened
and peace and concord may be established.

3

Why is man so hard of heart? It is because he does not yet know God. If he had knowledge of God he could not act in direct opposition to His laws; if he were spiritually minded such a line of conduct would be impossible to him. If only the laws and precepts of the prophets of God had been believed, understood and followed, wars would no longer darken the face of the earth.

4

All religions teach that we must do good, that we must be generous, sincere, truthful, law-abiding, and faithful; all this is reasonable, and logically the only way in which humanity can progress.

All religious laws conform to reason, and are suited to the people for whom they are framed, and for the age in which they are to be obeyed.

5

The members of the Government should consider the laws of God when they are framing plans for the ruling of the people. The general rights of mankind must be guarded and preserved.

6

The government of the countries should conform to the Divine Law which gives equal justice to all. This is the only way in which the deplorable superfluity of great wealth and miserable, demoralizing, degrading poverty can be abolished. Not until this is done will the Law of God be obeyed.

7

The object of punishment is not vengeance, but the prevention of crime.

8

You must endeavor always to live and act in direct obedience to the teachings and laws of Bahá'u'lláh, so that every individual may see in all the acts of your life that in word and in deed you are followers of the Blessed Perfection.

9

Through the power of faith, obey ye the teachings of God, and let all your actions conform to His laws. . . . [R]ise up as ye are bidden in the heavenly teachings. Thus may each one of you be even as a candle casting its light, the center of attraction wherever people come together; and from you, as from a bed of flowers, may sweet scents be shed.

10

All men are equal before the law, which must reign absolutely.

11

Today nothing short of these divine teachings can assure peace and tranquility to mankind. But for these teachings, this darkness shall never vanish, these chronic diseases shall never be healed; nay, they shall grow fiercer from day to day.

12

When the laws of the Most Holy Book are enforced, contentions and disputes will find a final sentence of absolute justice before a general tribunal of the nations and kingdoms, and the difficulties that appear will be solved.

13

Therefore, They [the Prophets or Manifestations of God] establish laws which are suitable and adapted to the state of the world of man, for religion is the essential connection which proceeds from the realities of things.

14

The central purpose of the divine religions is the establishment of peace and unity among mankind. Their reality is one; therefore, their accomplishment is one and universal—whether it be through the essential or material ordinances of God. There is but one light of the material sun, one ocean, one rain, one atmosphere.

15

The divine Prophets have revealed and founded religion. They have laid down certain laws and heavenly principles for the guidance of mankind. They have taught and promulgated the knowledge of God, established praiseworthy ethical ideals and inculcated the highest standards of virtues in the human world.

16

The Prophets of God, the supreme Manifestations, are like skilled physicians, and the contingent world is like the body of man: the divine laws are the remedy and treatment. Consequently, the doctor must be aware of, and know, all the members and parts, as well as the constitution and state of the patient, so that he can prescribe a medicine which will be beneficial against the violent poison of the disease. In reality the doctor deduces from the disease itself the treatment which is suited to the patient, for he diagnoses the malady, and afterward prescribes the remedy for the illness. Until the malady be discovered, how can the remedy and treatment be prescribed? The doctor then must have a thorough knowledge of the constitution, members, organs and state of the patient, and be acquainted with all diseases and all remedies, in order to prescribe a fitting medicine.

Religion, then, is the necessary connection which emanates from the reality of things; and as the supreme Manifestations of God are aware of the mysteries of beings, therefore, They understand this essential connection, and by this knowledge establish the Law of God.

17

The Prophets of God have founded the laws of divine civilization. They have been the root and fundamental source of all knowledge.

18

The essence of the Bahá'í spirit is that, in order to establish a better social order and economic condition, there must be allegiance to the laws and principles of government.

19

Laws for the ordinary conditions of life are only valid temporarily. The exigencies of the time of Moses justified cutting off a man's hand for theft, but such a penalty is not allowable now. Time changes conditions, and laws change to suit conditions. We must remember that these changing laws are not the essentials; they are the accidentals of religion. The essential ordinances established by a Manifestation of God are spiritual; they concern moralities, the ethical development of man and faith in God. They are ideal and necessarily permanent—expressions of the one foundation and not amenable to change or transformation. Therefore, the fundamental basis of the revealed religion of

God is immutable, unchanging throughout the centuries, not subject to the varying conditions of the human world.

20

Each of the divine religions contains two kinds of laws or ordinances. One division concerns the world of morality and ethical institutions. These are the essential ordinances. They instill and awaken the knowledge and love of God, love for humanity, the virtues of the world of mankind, the attributes of the divine Kingdom, rebirth and resurrection from the kingdom of nature. These constitute one kind of divine law which is common to all and never subject to change. From the dawn of the Adamic cycle to the present day this fundamental law of God has continued changeless. This is the foundation of divine religion.

The second division comprises laws and institutions which provide for human needs and conditions according to exigencies of time and place. These are accidental, of no essential importance and should never have been made the cause and source of human contention.

21

Christ appeared in order to illumine the world of humanity, to render the earthly world celestial, to make the human kingdom a realm of angels, to unite the hearts, to enkindle the light of love in human souls, so that such souls might become independent, attaining complete unity and fellowship, turning to God, entering into the divine Kingdom, receiving the bounties and bestowals of God and partaking of the manna from heaven. Through Christ they were intended to be baptized by the Holy Spirit, attain a new spirit and realize the everlasting life. All the holy precepts and the announcements of prophetic laws were for these various and heavenly purposes.

22

Investigation of the one fundamental reality and allegiance to the essential unchanging principles of the Word of God can alone establish unity and love in human hearts.

23

Consider whether there exists anywhere in creation a principle mightier in every sense than religion, or whether any conceivable power is more pervasive than the various Divine Faiths, or whether any agency can bring about real love and fellowship and union among all peoples as can belief in an almighty and all-knowing God, or whether except for the laws of God there has been any evidence of an instrumentality for educating all mankind in every phase of righteousness.

24

In this wondrous age . . . praised be God, the commandments of God are not delimited, not restricted to any one group of people, rather have all the friends been commanded to show forth fellowship and love, consideration and generosity and loving-kindness to every community on earth. Now must the lovers of God arise to carry out these instructions of His: let them be kindly fathers to the children of the human race, and compassionate brothers to the youth, and self-denying offspring to those bent with years. The meaning of this is that ye must show forth tenderness and love to every human being, even to your enemies, and welcome them all with unalloyed friendship, good cheer, and loving-kindness.

25

O my Lord and my Hope! Help Thou Thy loved ones to be steadfast in Thy mighty Covenant, to remain faithful to Thy manifest Cause, and to carry out the commandments Thou didst set down for them in Thy Book of Splendors; that they may become banners of guidance and lamps of the Company above, wellsprings of Thine infinite wisdom, and stars that lead aright, as they shine down from the supernal sky.

Verily art Thou the Invincible, the Almighty, the All-Powerful.

26

But if man lives up to these divine commandments, this world of earth shall be transformed into the world of heaven, and this material sphere shall be converted into a paradise of glory.

27

Religion is the light of the world, and the progress, achievement, and happiness of man result from obedience to the laws set down in the holy Books.

28

Love and obey your Heavenly Father, and rest assured that Divine help is yours.

29

We must obey God, and strive to follow Him by leaving all our prejudices and bringing about peace on earth.

30

The Faith of the Blessed Beauty is summoning mankind to safety and love, to amity and peace; it hath raised up its tabernacle on the heights of the earth, and directeth its call to all nations. Wherefore, O ye who are God's lovers, know ye the value of this precious Faith, obey its teachings, walk in this road that is drawn straight, and show ye this way to the people. Lift up your voices and sing out the song of the Kingdom. Spread far and wide the precepts and counsels of the loving Lord, so that this world will change into another world, and this darksome earth will be flooded with light, and the dead body of mankind will arise and live; so that every soul will ask for immortality, through the holy breaths of God.

31

The flag of freedom and banner of liberty have been unfurled here, but the prosperity and advancement of a city, the happiness and greatness of a country depend upon its hearing and obeying the call of God. The light of reality must shine therein and divine civilization be founded; then the radiance of the Kingdom will be diffused and heavenly influences surround. Material civilization is likened to the body, whereas divine civilization is the spirit in that body.

32

All are commanded to seek the good pleasure of the Lord of unity, to follow His command and obey His will; in this way the world of humanity shall become illumined with the reality of love and reconciliation.

33

The whole earth is one home, and all peoples, did they but know it, are bathed in the oneness of God's mercy. God created all. He gives sustenance to all. He guides and trains all under the shadow of his bounty. We must follow the example God Himself gives us, and do away with all disputations and quarrels.

34

God sent His Prophets into the world to teach and enlighten man, to explain to him the mystery of the Power of the Holy Spirit, to enable him to reflect the light, and so in his turn, to be the source of guidance to others. The Heavenly Books, the Bible, the Qur'án, and the other Holy Writings have been given by God as guides into the paths of Divine virtue, love, justice and peace.

Therefore I say unto you that ye should strive to follow the counsels of these Blessed Books, and so order your lives that ye may, following the examples set before you, become yourselves the saints of the Most High!

35

If in this day a soul shall act according to the precepts and the counsels of God, he will serve as a divine physician to mankind, and like the trump of Israfil,* he will call the dead of this contingent world to life; for the confirmations of the Abhá Realm† are never interrupted, and such a virtuous soul hath, to befriend him, the unfailing help of the Company on high. Thus shall a sorry gnat become an eagle in the fullness of his strength, and a feeble sparrow change to a royal falcon in the heights of ancient glory.

---

* Believed to be the angel appointed to sound the trumpet on the Day of Resurrection to raise the dead at the bidding of the Lord.
† *Most Glorious Realm;* the world beyond this one.

36

Act in accordance with the counsels of the Lord: that is, rise up in such wise, and with such qualities, as to endow the body of this world with a living soul, and to bring this young child, humanity, to the stage of adulthood.

37

Every divine Manifestation is the very life of the world, and the skilled physician of each ailing soul. The world of man is sick, and that competent Physician knoweth the cure, arising as He doth with teachings, counsels and admonishments that are the remedy for every pain, the healing balm to every wound.

38

If we do not seek the counsel of God or if we refuse to follow His dictates, it is presumptive evidence that we are knowing and wise, whereas God is ignorant; that we are sagacious and God is not. God forbid! We seek shelter in His mercy for this suggestion! No matter how far the human intelligence may advance, it is still but a drop, while divine omniscience is the ocean.

39

If you abide by the precepts and teachings of the Blessed Perfection, the heavenly world and ancient Kingdom will be yours—eternal happiness, love and everlasting life.

40

Make firm our steps, O Lord, in Thy path and strengthen Thou our hearts in Thine obedience. Turn our faces toward the beauty of Thy oneness, and gladden our bosoms with the signs of Thy divine unity. Adorn our bodies with the robe of Thy bounty, and remove from our eyes the veil of sinfulness, and give us the chalice of Thy grace; that the essence of all beings may sing Thy praise before the vision of Thy grandeur. Reveal then Thyself, O Lord, by Thy merciful utterance and the mystery of Thy divine being, that the holy ecstasy of prayer may fill our souls—a prayer that shall rise above words and letters and transcend the murmur of syllables and sounds—that all things may be merged into nothingness before the revelation of Thy splendor.

Lord! These are servants that have remained fast and firm in Thy Covenant and Thy Testament, that have held fast unto the cord of constancy in Thy Cause and clung unto the hem of the robe of Thy grandeur. Assist them, O Lord, with Thy grace, confirm with Thy power and strengthen their loins in obedience to Thee.

Thou art the Pardoner, the Gracious.

41

O compassionate God! Thanks be to Thee for Thou hast awakened and made me conscious. Thou hast given me a seeing eye and favored me with a hearing ear, hast led me to Thy kingdom and guided me to Thy path. Thou hast shown me the right way and caused me to enter the ark of deliverance. O God! Keep me steadfast and make me firm and staunch. Protect me from violent tests, and preserve and shelter me in the strongly fortified fortress of Thy Covenant and Testament. Thou art the Powerful. Thou art the Seeing. Thou art the Hearing.

O Thou the Compassionate God. Bestow upon me a heart which, like unto glass, may be illumined with the light of Thy love, and confer upon me thoughts which may change this world into a rose garden through the outpourings of heavenly grace.

Thou art the Compassionate, the Merciful. Thou art the Great Beneficent God.

42

It is your duty to be exceedingly kind to every human being, and to wish him well; to work for the upliftment of society; to blow the breath of life into the dead; to act in accordance with the instructions of Bahá'u'lláh and walk His path—until ye change the world of man into the world of God.

43

O my spiritual loved ones! Praise be to God, ye have thrust the veils aside and recognized the compassionate Beloved, and have hastened away from this abode to the placeless realm. Ye have pitched your tents in the world of God, and to glorify Him, the Self-Subsistent, ye have raised sweet voices and sung songs that pierced the heart. Well done! A thousand times well done! For ye have beheld the Light made manifest, and in your reborn beings ye have raised the cry, "Blessed be the Lord, the best of all creators!" Ye were but babes in the womb, then were ye sucklings, and from a precious breast ye drew the milk of knowledge, then came ye to your full growth, and won salvation. Now is the time for service, and for servitude unto the Lord. Release yourselves from all distracting thoughts, deliver the Message with an eloquent tongue, adorn your assemblages with praise of the Beloved, till bounty shall descend in overwhelming floods and dress the world in fresh greenery and blossoms. This streaming bounty is even the counsels, admonitions, instructions, and injunctions of Almighty God.

44

Just as God loves all and is kind to all, so must we really love and be kind to everybody. We must consider none bad, none worthy of detestation, no one as an enemy. We must love all; nay, we must consider everyone as related to us, for all are the servants of one God. All are under the instructions of one Educator.

45

Today the world of humanity is walking in darkness because it is out of touch with the world of God. That is why we do not see the signs of God in the hearts of men. The power of the Holy Spirit has no influence. When a divine spiritual illumination becomes manifest in the world of humanity, when divine instruction and guidance appear, then enlightenment follows, a new spirit is realized within, a new power descends, and a new life is given.

46

The greatest bestowal of God in the world of humanity is religion, for assuredly the divine teachings of religion are above all other sources of instruction and development to man. Religion confers upon man eternal life and guides his footsteps in the world of morality. It opens the doors of unending happiness and bestows everlasting honor upon the human kingdom. It has been the basis of all civilization and progress in the history of mankind.

47

Universal benefits derive from the grace of the Divine religions, for they lead their true followers to sincerity of intent, to high purpose, to purity and spotless honor, to surpassing kindness and compassion, to the keeping of their covenants when they have covenanted, to concern for the rights of others, to liberality, to justice in every aspect of life, to humanity and philanthropy, to valor and to unflagging efforts in the service of mankind. It is religion, to sum up, which produces all human virtues, and it is these virtues which are the bright candles of civilization. . . .

The purpose of these statements is to make it abundantly clear that the Divine religions, the holy precepts, the heavenly teachings, are the un-assailable basis of human happiness, and that the peoples of the world can hope for no real relief or deliverance without this one great remedy.

48

I ask you all, each one of you, to follow well the light of truth, in the Holy Teachings, and God will strengthen you by His Holy Spirit so that you will be enabled to overcome the difficulties, and to destroy the prejudices which cause separation and hatred amongst the people. Let your hearts be filled with the great love of God, let it be felt by all; for every man is a servant of God, and all are entitled to a share of the Divine Bounty.

49

Our greatest efforts must be directed towards detachment from the things of the world; we must strive to become more spiritual, more luminous, to follow the counsel of the Divine Teaching, to serve the cause of unity and true equality, to be merciful, to reflect the love of the Highest on all men, so that the light of the Spirit shall be apparent in all our deeds, to the end that all humanity shall be united, the stormy sea thereof calmed, and all rough waves disappear from off the surface of life's ocean henceforth unruffled and peaceful.

NOTES

From the Writings of Bahá'u'lláh

1. *Gleanings from the Writings of Bahá'u'lláh,* no. 155.3.
2. Kitáb-i-Aqdas, ¶1.
3. *Gems of Divine Mysteries,* p. 13.
4. *Gleanings from the Writings of Bahá'u'lláh,* no. 102.1.
5. The Seven Valleys, p. 64.
6. *Gems of Divine Mysteries,* p. 9.
7. *Gleanings from the Writings of Bahá'u'lláh,* no. 138.1.
8. Ibid., no. 94.2.
9. Kitáb-i-Aqdas, ¶81.

10. *Gleanings from the Writings of Bahá'u'lláh,* no. 113.23.

11. *Bahá'í Prayers,* p. 261.

12. *Gleanings from the Writings of Bahá'u'lláh,* no. 114.21.

13. Ibid., no. 161.1.

14. *Prayers and Meditations,* p. 14.

15. Ibid., p. 27.

16. Ibid., p. 105.

17. *Tablets of Bahá'u'lláh,* p. 129.

18. Kitáb-i-Íqán, ¶47.

19. *The Summons of the Lord of Hosts,* no. 1.152.

20. *Epistle to the Son of the Wolf,* p. 13.

21. *Gems of Divine Mysteries,* p. 33.

22. *Gleanings from the Writings of Bahá'u'lláh,* no. 65.3.

23. Ibid., no. 118.8.

24. *Prayers and Meditations,* p. 283.

25. *Gleanings from the Writings of Bahá'u'lláh,* no. 133.2.

26. Ibid., no. 138.2.

27. Kitáb-i-Aqdas, ¶5.

28. Ibid., ¶7.

29. *Tablets of Bahá'u'lláh,* p. 93.

30. Ibid., p. 251.

31. Kitáb-i-Aqdas, ¶4.

32. *Bahá'í Prayers,* pp. 184–85.

33. Kitáb-i-Aqdas, ¶29.

34. Ibid., ¶45.

35. Ibid., ¶96.

36. *The Summons of the Lord of Hosts,* no. 1.237.

37. *Gleanings from the Writings of Bahá'u'lláh,* no. 155.4.

38. Ibid., no. 59.5.

39. Ibid., no. 133.1.

40. Ibid., no. 139.8.

41. Ibid., no. 159.4.

42. *Tablets of Bahá'u'lláh,* p. 126.

43. Ibid., p. 267.

44. The Hidden Words, Arabic, no. 39.

45. *Tablets of Bahá'u'lláh,* p. 155.

From the Writings of the Báb

1. *Selections from the Writings of the Báb,* no. 3.4.1.
2. Ibid., no. 3.14.1.
3. Ibid., no. 2.3.5.
4. Ibid., no. 5.10.1.
5. Ibid., no. 5.19.2.
6. *Bahá'í Prayers,* pp. 226–27.

From the Writings and Recorded Utterances of 'Abdu'l-Bahá

1. *Paris Talks,* no. 47.1.
2. Ibid., no. 34.6.
3. Ibid., no. 37.5.
4. Ibid., no. 44.5–6.
5. Ibid., no. 46.12.
6. Ibid., no. 46.13.
7. Ibid., no. 47.3.
8. Ibid., no. 52.3.
9. *Selections from the Writings of 'Abdu'l-Bahá,* no. 17.3.
10. *Paris Talks,* no. 47.2.

11. *Selections from the Writings of 'Abdu'l-Bahá*, no. 202.14.

12. *Some Answered Questions*, p. 64.

13. Ibid., p. 158.

14. *The Promulgation of Universal Peace*, p. 135.

15. Ibid., p. 192.

16. *Some Answered Questions*, pp. 158–59.

17. *The Promulgation of Universal Peace*, p. 194.

18. Ibid., p. 333.

19. Ibid., p. 516.

20. Ibid., pp. 553–54.

21. Ibid., p. 624.

22. Ibid., p. 628.

23. *The Secret of Divine Civilization*, ¶150.

24. *Selections from the Writings of 'Abdu'l-Bahá*, no. 7.4.

25. Ibid., no. 206.16–17.

26. *The Promulgation of Universal Peace*, p. 663.

27. *The Secret of Divine Civilization*, ¶130.

28. *Paris Talks*, no. 32.14.

29. Ibid., no. 40.21.

30. *Selections from the Writings of 'Abdu'l-Bahá,* no. 1.6.

31. *The Promulgation of Universal Peace,* p. 143.

32. Ibid., pp. 449–50.

33. *'Abdu'l-Bahá in London,* p. 38.

34. *Paris Talks,* no. 18.6–7.

35. *Selections from the Writings of 'Abdu'l-Bahá,* no. 8.4.

36. Ibid., no. 16.5.

37. Ibid., no. 29.4.

38. *The Promulgation of Universal Peace,* p. 91.

39. Ibid., p. 11.

40. *Bahá'í Prayers,* pp. 69–70.

41. Ibid., p. 70.

42. *Selections from the Writings of 'Abdu'l-Bahá,* no. 47.4.

43. Ibid., no. 236.4.

44. *The Promulgation of Universal Peace,* p. 373.

45. Ibid., p. 424.

46. Ibid., p. 510.

47. *The Secret of Divine Civilization,* ¶173–74.
48. *Paris Talks,* no. 5.24.
49. Ibid., no. 104–5.

BIBLIOGRAPHY

Works of Bahá'u'lláh

Epistle to the Son of the Wolf. New ed. Translated by Shoghi Effendi. 1st ps ed. Wilmette, IL: Bahá'í Publishing Trust, 1988.

Gleanings from the Writings of Bahá'u'lláh. Translated by Shoghi Effendi. Wilmette, IL: Bahá'í Publishing, 2005.

The Hidden Words. Translated by Shoghi Effendi. Wilmette, IL: Bahá'í Publishing, 2002.

The Kitáb-i-Aqdas: The Most Holy Book. 1st ps ed. Wilmette, IL: Bahá'í Publishing Trust, 1993.

The Kitáb-i-Íqán: The Book of Certitude. Translated by Shoghi Effendi. Wilmette, IL: Bahá'í Publishing, 2003.

The Pen of Glory: Selected Works of Bahá'u'lláh. Wilmette, IL: Bahá'í Publishing, 2008.

Prayers and Meditations. Translated by Shoghi Effendi. 1st pocket-size ed. Wilmette, IL: Bahá'í Publishing Trust, 1987.

The Seven Valleys and the Four Valleys. New ed. Translated by Ali-Kuli Khan and Marzieh Gail. Wilmette, IL: Bahá'í Publishing Trust, 1991.

The Summons of the Lord of Hosts: Tablets of Bahá'u'lláh. Wilmette, IL: Bahá'í Publishing, 2006.

Tablets of Bahá'u'lláh revealed after the Kitáb-i-Aqdas. Compiled by the Research Department of the Universal House of Justice. Translated by Habib Taherzadeh et al. Wilmette, IL: Bahá'í Publishing Trust, 1988.

Works of the Báb

Selections from the Writings of the Báb. Compiled by the Research Department of the Universal House of Justice. Translated by Habib Taherzadeh et al. Wilmette, IL: Bahá'í Publishing Trust, 2006.

Works of 'Abdu'l-Bahá

'Abdu'l-Bahá in London: Addresses & Notes of Conversations. London: Bahá'í Publishing Trust, 1987.

Paris Talks: Addresses Given By 'Abdu'l-Bahá in Paris in 1911. Wilmette, IL: Bahá'í Publishing, 2011.

Promulgation of Universal Peace: Talks Delivered by 'Abdu'l-Bahá during His Visit to the United States and Canada in 1912. Compiled by Howard MacNutt. Wilmette, IL: Bahá'í Publishing, 2012.

The Secret of Divine Civilization. Translated by Marzieh Gail and Ali-Kuli Khan. Wilmette, IL: Bahá'í Publishing, 2007.

Selections from the Writings of 'Abdu'l-Bahá. Compiled by the Research Department of the Universal House of Justice. Translated by a Committee at the Bahá'í World Center and Marzieh Gail. Wilmette, IL: Bahá'í Publishing, 2010.

Some Answered Questions. Compiled and translated by Laura Clifford Barney. 1st pocket-size ed. Wilmette, IL: Bahá'í Publishing Trust, 1984.

Bahá'í Compilations

Bahá'í Prayers: A Selection of Prayers Revealed by Bahá'u'lláh, the Báb, and 'Abdu'l-Bahá. Wilmette, IL: Bahá'í Publishing Trust, 2008.

Bahá'í PUBLISHING

Bahá'í Publishing and the Bahá'í Faith

Bahá'í Publishing produces books based on the teachings of the Bahá'í Faith. Founded over 160 years ago, the Bahá'í Faith has spread to some 235 nations and territories and is now accepted by more than five million people. The word "Bahá'í" means "follower of Bahá'u'lláh." Bahá'u'lláh, the founder of the Bahá'í Faith, asserted that He is the Messenger of God for all of humanity in this day. The cornerstone of His teachings is the establishment of the spiritual unity of humankind, which will be achieved by personal transformation and the application of clearly identified spiritual principles. Bahá'ís also believe that there is but one religion and that all the Messengers of God—among them Abraham, Zoroaster, Moses, Krishna, Buddha, Jesus, and Muḥammad—have progressively revealed its nature. Together, the world's great religions are expressions of a single, unfolding divine plan. Human beings, not God's Messengers, are the source of religious divisions, prejudices, and hatreds.

The Bahá'í Faith is not a sect or denomination of another religion, nor is it a cult or a social movement. Rather, it is a globally recognized independent world religion founded on new books of scripture revealed by Bahá'u'lláh.

Bahá'í Publishing is an imprint of the National Spiritual Assembly of the Bahá'ís of the United States.

For more information about the Bahá'í Faith,
or to contact Bahá'ís near you,
visit http://www.bahai.us/
or call
1-800-22-UNITE

Other Books Available from
Bahá'í Publishing

RETRIEVING OUR SPIRITUAL HERITAGE

Bahá'í Chair for World Peace:
Lectures and Essays, 1994–2005
Suheil Bushrui
$20.00 US / $22.00 CAN
Hardcover
ISBN 978-1-61851-016-7

A collection of lectures and essays that place interfaith dialogue, the oneness of humanity, and the human spirit at the heart of public discourse.

In *Retrieving Our Spiritual Heritage,* Professor Bushrui calls for interfaith dialog and focuses on some of the timeless shared values of many of the world's religions—such as love, selflessness, and generosity—but also delves into how these values can be applied to the many conflicts and crises facing the world today. Covering such topics as education, globalization, peace, and the environment, Professor Bushrui evokes the timeless wisdom of the world's religions as well as the voices of the poets and scholars of the past, addressing his subject matter at the level of high principle and universal values. The result is a deeply moving and thought-provoking call to humanity to place the human spirit at the heart of discourse concerning the vital issues of our time.

TALKS BY 'ABDU'L-BAHÁ

THE SPIRIT OF CHRIST

'Abdu'l-Bahá

$14.00 US / $16.00 CAN

Hardcover

ISBN 978-1-61851-020-4

A spiritually uplifting and thought-provoking collection of talks that pay tribute to the spirit of Jesus Christ and the significance of His teachings and station.

Talks by 'Abdu'l-Bahá: The Spirit of Christ is a collection of talks given by 'Abdu'l-Bahá during his historic journey through Europe and North America in 1911 and 1912. As the son and appointed successor of Bahá'u'lláh, the Prophet and Founder of the Bahá'í Faith, 'Abdu'l-Bahá spoke extensively to a wide range of audiences and offered profound insights on a diversity of subjects. This volume specifically highlights talks that deal with the spirit of Christ, and the impact that His life and teachings had on the world. In these talks, readers will find glowing tributes to the station of Christ, Whom Bahá'ís revere as a divinely inspired Messenger of God.

BAHÁ'Í BASICS

A Guide to the Beliefs, Practices, and History of the Bahá'í Faith

Frances Worthington

$14.00 US / $16.00 CAN

Trade Paper

ISBN 978-1-61851-017-4

An introduction to the Bahá'í Faith that covers the basic teachings, principles, and history of the Faith in an easy-to-use Q&A format.

In *Baháʼí Basics,* author Frances Worthington uses a simple and accessible format that highlights the clarity with which many of the topics associated with the Bahá'í Faith are discussed. The result is a basic and informational introduction to what is one of the fastest growing religions in the world. In most cases the answers are presented using direct quotations from the central figures of the Faith—Baháʼuʼlláh, the Báb, ʻAbduʼl-Bahá—as well as Shoghi Effendi and the Universal House of Justice. Readers will find themselves well-informed after reading this concise, well-organized introduction, which provides clear, straightforward answers to the basic questions that arise when investigating a new religion.

THE HIDDEN WORDS

Bahá'u'lláh

$14.00 US / $16.00 CAN

Hardcover

ISBN 978-1-61851-018-1

A collection of lyrical, gem-like verses that convey timeless spiritual wisdom and represent one of the most important and cherished scriptural works of the Bahá'í Faith.

The Hidden Words is a collection of 153 gem-like verses revealed by Bahá'u'lláh—the Prophet and Founder of the Bahá'í Faith—in 1858 while meditating and walking the banks of the Tigris River in Baghdad, Iraq. Representing one of the most important and cherished scriptural works of the Bahá'í Faith, the verses are a perfect guidebook to walking a spiritual path and drawing closer to God. They address themes such as turning to God, humility, detachment, and love, to name but a few. These verses are among Bahá'u'lláh's earliest and best-known works, having been translated into more than seventy languages and read by millions worldwide. The interior design of this title includes a short passage on each page, encouraging the reader to think and to meditate.